SMART AND EASY BB[...] RECI[...]

Take Your Favorite Restaurant at Home Becoming The Master Chef Your Family Will Love. Spoil Everybody With Delicious, Various, and Easy-to-Copy recipes.

BY

RONALD MURPHY

including, but not limited to, - errors, omissions, or inaccuracies.

contents

introduction

There are various types of Bread machine. Schemes differ in the number of fasting days and calorie limits. Bread machine requires wholly or partly refraining from food for a certain period before eating normally again. It is suggested by the proponents of this type of diet that it can offer weight-loss, improved fitness, and longer lifespans. Proponents of this diet contend that an Bread machine regimen is more straightforward to manage than conventional calorie-controlled meals. Each individual's experience of Bread machine is different, and different ways are suitable for different people. There are numerous ways of Bread machine, and people may choose any of them according to their choice. Keep reading to find out about different ways of doing Bread machine.

Type 1: Fasting 12 hours in a Day The guidelines for this diet are straightforward. An individual is required to determine and stick to a 12-hour fasting period every day. According to several researchers, fast for 10–16 hours may cause the body to transform its stored fat into energy that moves ketones into the bloodstream. Its purpose is to promote weight loss. This form of Bread machine program can be an excellent opportunity for beginners. That is because the fasting duration is relatively short, a lot of fasting happens during sleep, and a person can eat the same number of calories every day. The best way to do the 12-hour fast is to include the time of sleep or rest in the fasting time frame. For instance, someone may select to fast between 7 p.m. to 7 a.m. in the next morning. He would need to end his dinner before 7 p.m. Then he would wait till 7 a.m. To eat breakfast, he can sleep for a lot of time in between.

Baked Apples

Servings Provided: 4

Macro Counts Per Serving:
- **Calories**: 175
- **Protein**: 7 g
- **Fat Content**: 20 g
- **Total Net Carbs**: 16g

Ingredient List:
- Keto-friendly sweetener (4 tsp. or to taste)
- Cinnamon (.75 tsp.)
- Chopped pecans (.25 cup)
- Granny Smith apples (4 large)

Prep Technique:

1. Set the oven temperature at 375°
Fahrenheit.
2. Mix the sweetener with the
cinnamon and pecans.
3. Core the apple and add the
prepared stuffing.
4. Add enough water into the baking
dish to cover the bottom of the
apple.
5. Bake for about 45 minutes to 1
hour.

Chocolate Dipped Candied Bacon

Servings Provided: 16
Macro Counts Per Serving:
- **Calories**: 54
- **Protein**: 3 g
- **Fat Content**: 4.1 g
- **Total Net Carbs**: 1.1 g
Ingredient List:
- Thin-cut slices of bacon (16)
- Brown sugar alternative – ex. Sukrin Gold or erythritol (2 tbsp.)
- Cinnamon (.5 tsp.)

- Cacao butter (.5 oz.) or coconut oil (1 tbsp.)
- 85% dark chocolate (3 oz.)
- Sugar-free maple extract (1 tsp.)

Prep Technique:

1. Mix the Sukrin Gold sweetener with the cinnamon.

2. Lay the strips of bacon onto a parchment paper-lined tray. Sprinkle with half of the mixture.

3. Turn them over and do the other side with the rest of the mix.

4. Heat up the oven to reach 275° Fahrenheit. Bake until caramelized and crispy (60 to 75 min.).

5. Warm a pan to melt the cocoa butter and chocolate. Pour the maple syrup into the mixture and stir well. Set to the side until it's room temperature.

6. Arrange the bacon on a platter to cool thoroughly before dipping into the chocolate.

7. Dip half of each strip of bacon in the chocolate. Place on a tray for the chocolate to solidify. You can place it in the fridge or just on the countertop.

Cinnamon Vanilla Protein Bites

Servings Provided: 18-20 bites
Macro Counts Per Serving:
- **Calories**: 112
- **Protein**: 2 g
- **Fat Content**: 9 g
- **Total Net Carbs**: 4 g

Ingredient List:
- Quick oats (.75 cup)
- Nut butter of choice (.25 - .33 cup)
- Cinnamon (1 tbsp.)
- Pure maple syrup (.25 - .33 cup)
- Vanilla protein powder (.25 cup)

- Almond meal (.5 cup)
- Vanilla extract (.5 - 1 tsp.)
- *Also Needed:* Food processor

Prep Technique:

1. Line a cookie tin with a layer of parchment paper.
2. Grind the oats with the processor and add to a mixing container. Combine the cinnamon, protein powder, almond meal, and nut butter.
3. Mix in the syrup and vanilla. Using your hands, mix well, and roll into
small balls.
4. Freeze for 20 to 30 minutes.
5. Store in a Ziploc-type baggie with the cinnamon and vanilla protein mixture.

Guacamole Deviled Eggs

Servings Provided: 8
Macro Counts Per Serving:
- **Calories**: 119
- **Protein**: 4.2g
- **Fat Content**: 9.9 g
- **Total Net Carbs**: 5g

Ingredient List:
- Eggs (4 in the shell)
- Minced green onion (1 tbsp.)
- Chopped cilantro (1 tbsp.)
- Avocados (2 peeled, pitted, and mashed)
- Fresh lime juice (2 tsp.)
- Seeded jalapeno pepper (2 tsp.)

- Hot pepper sauce (dash Tabasco)
- Salt (.5 tsp.)
- Dijon-style mustard (1 tsp.)
- Worcestershire sauce (1 tsp.)
- Paprika (1 pinch)

Prep Technique:

1. Gently arrange the eggs in a saucepan – covered with clean water. Place a lid on the pot, and let it simmer for 10-12 minutes.

2. Transfer the eggs from the pot and let them cool in a container of cold water. When chilled, slice into halves and add the yolks to a mixing container. Toss in the cilantro, avocado, jalapeno, and onion.

3. Stir in the juice along with the mustard, Worcestershire sauce, salt, and hot sauce. Blend well.

4. Fill the egg white halves and stick in the fridge until ready to eat.

5. Sprinkle using the paprika.

Beef and Broccoli - Slow Cooked

Servings Provided: 4
Macro Counts Per Serving:
- **Calories**: 430
- **Protein**: 54 g
- **Fat Content**: 19 g
- **Total Net Carbs**: 3 g

Ingredient List:
- Liquid aminos (.66 cup)
- Flank steak (2 lb.)
- Beef broth (1 cup)
- Freshly grated ginger (1 tsp.)
- Keto-friendly sweetener - your choice (3 tbsp.)

- Minced garlic (3 cloves)
- Salt (.5 tsp.)
- Red pepper flakes (.5 tsp. or to taste)
- Broccoli (1 head)
- Red bell pepper (1)

Prep Technique:

1. Program the cooker using the low heat setting.
2. Slice the steak and into one to two-inch chunks.
3. Pour in the beef broth, aminos, steak, ginger, sweetener, garlic cloves,
salt, and red pepper flakes.
4. Cook five to six hours on the low setting.
5. Slice the red pepper into one-inch pieces, and slice the broccoli into florets. After the steak is cooked, stir well.
6. Toss in the peppers and broccoli on top of everything in the slow

cooker. Continue cooking for at least one more hour.

7. Add everything together, and sprinkle with sesame seeds for topping.

Cheeseburger Calzone

Servings Provided: 8

Macro Counts Per Serving:

- **Calories**: 580
- **Protein**: 34 g
- **Fat Content**: 47 g
- **Total Net Carbs**: 3 g

Ingredient List:

- Dill pickle spears (4)
- Cream cheese – divided (8 oz.)
- Shredded mozzarella cheese (1 cup)
- Egg (1)

- Yellow diced onion (.5 of 1)
- Ground beef - lean (1.5 lb.)
- Thick-cut bacon strips (4)
- Mayonnaise (.5 cup)
- Shredded cheddar cheese (1 cup)
- Almond flour (1 cup)

Prep Technique:

1. Program the oven temperature setting to 425° Fahrenheit. Prepare a
cookie tin with parchment paper.

2. Chop the pickles into spears. Set aside for now.

3. Prepare the crust. Combine about half of the cream cheese and mozzarella cheese. Microwave 35 seconds. When it melts, add the egg and almond flour to make the dough. Set aside.

4. Cook the beef on the stove using the medium heat setting.

5. Prepare the bacon until crunchy (microwave for five minutes or

stovetop). When cool, break into bits.

6. Dice the onion and add to the beef. Cook until softened. Toss in the

bacon, cheddar cheese, pickle bits, the rest of the cream cheese, and mayonnaise. Stir well.

7. Roll the dough onto the prepared baking tin. Scoop the mixture into the

center. Fold the ends and side to make the calzone.

8. Bake until browned or about 15 minutes. Let it rest for 10 minutes before slicing.

Cube Steak- Instant Pot

Servings Provided: 8
Macro Counts Per Serving:
- **Calories**: 154
- **Protein**: 23.5 g
- **Fat Content**: 5.5 g
- **Total Net Carbs**: 3 g

Ingredient List:
- Water (1 cup)
- Cubed steaks(8- 28 oz. pkg.)
- Black pepper (as desired)
- Garlic salt/adobo seasoning (1.75 tsp.)
- Tomato sauce (8 oz. can)
- Green pitted olives (.33 cup) + the brine (2 tbsp.)
- Red pepper (1 small)
- Medium onion (.5 of 1 or 2 small)

Prep Technique:
1. Chop the peppers and onions into ¼-inch strips.

2. Prepare the beef with the salt/adobo and pepper. Toss into the Instant
Pot with the remainder of the fixings.
3. Secure the top and prepare for 25 minutes under high pressure. Natural
release the pressure and serve.

Oven-Roasted Burgers

Servings Provided: 4
Macro Counts Per Serving:
- **Calories**: 262
- **Protein**: 19 g
- **Fat Content**: 18 g
- **Total Net Carbs**: 4 g

Ingredient List:
- Thinly sliced onion (.5 of 1)
- Ground beef (1 lb.)
- Garlic powder (1 tsp.)
- Black pepper (1 tsp.)
- Onion powder (1 tsp.)
- Salt (1 tsp.)
- American cheese (2 slices)
- *Optional for Serving*: 1 sliced avocado/tomato

Prep Technique:
1. Set the oven to 400° Fahrenheit.
2. Use aluminum foil to cover a baking tin.
3. Combine the beef and seasonings (salt, pepper, onion powder, and

garlic powder). Shape into four patties and place them into the pan.

4. Bake one side for ten minutes and flip. Continue cooking until done (ten more minutes) and add the cheese and onions.

5. Cook five more minutes and serve with some tomato or avocado slices.

Note: The carbs are not calculated into the recipe nutritional information.

Slow-Cooked Steak Tacos

Servings Provided: 4
Macro Counts Per Serving:
- **Calories**: 196
- **Protein**: 25g
- **Fat Content**: 8 g
- **Total Net Carbs**: 4 g

Ingredient List:
- Chopped onion (.5 of 1)
- Bay leaves (1-2)
- Garlic cloves (4)
- Ancho chili powder (1.5 tsp.)
- Smoked paprika (1.5 tsp.)
- Salt and ground black pepper (.5 tsp. each)
- Beef broth (.5 cup)
- Tri-tip roast (1 lb.)

Prep Technique:
1. Remove the fat from the roast.
2. Mince the garlic into a paste using a garlic press or a food processor. You can also use the back of a knife and some coarse sea salt.

3. Combine the salt, pepper, chili powder, and paprika together to form a
rub. Coat the meat.
4. Toss in the onions and empty the beef broth into the slow cooker, adding the meat last. Cook eight hours using the low setting.
5. Remove the lid and shred the meat about 30 minutes from the end of
the cycle (7.5 hrs.). Leave the cover off to simmer for the last 30 minutes.
6. Serve as a lettuce wrap or other favorite choice.

Stuffed Meatloaf

Servings Provided: 8
Macro Counts Per Serving:
- **Calories**: 248.6
- **Protein**: 15.8 g
- **Fat Content**: 19.56 g
- **Total Net Carbs**: 1.42 g

Ingredient List:
- Cheddar cheese (6 slices)
- Ground beef (1.75 lb.)
- Spinach (.25 cup)
- Mushrooms (.25 cup)
- Green onions (.25 cup)
- Yellow onions (.25 cup)

Ingredient List - As Desired:
- Cumin
- Garlic
- Salt
- Pepper

Prep Technique:
1. Warm the oven to 350° Fahrenheit.

2. Combine the meat with the garlic and spices to your liking.
3. Grease a meatloaf pan. Leave the center open for the stuffing.
4. Chop the onions and combine with the mushrooms and spinach.
5. Mix a portion of the beef over the top with a layer of spinach, and mushrooms (for the top).
6. Bake one hour and enjoy it.

Taco Cabbage Skillet

Servings Provided: 4
Macro Counts Per Serving:
- **Calories**: 325
- **Protein**: 30 g
- **Fat Content**: 21 g
- **Total Net Carbs**: 4 g

Ingredient List:
- Ground beef (1 lb.)
- Salsa - ex. Pace Organic (.5 cup)
- Shredded cabbage (2 cups)
- Chili powder (2 tsp.)
- Shredded cheese (.75 cup)
- Salt and pepper (as desired)
- *Optional Garnishes*: Sour cream and green onions

Prep Technique:
1. Brown the beef and drain the fat. Pour in the salsa, cabbage, and seasoning.
2. Cover and lower the heat. Simmer for 10-12 minutes using the medium heat setting.

3. When the cabbage has softened, extinguish the heat and mix in the cheese.
4. Garnish with your favorite toppings and serve.

Grilled Pork Kebabs

Servings Provided: 4

Macro Counts Per Serving:

- **Protein**: 34 g
- **Fat Content**: 9 g
- **Total Net Carbs**: 3.3 g

Ingredient List:

- Hot sauce (2 tsp.)
- Sunflower seed butter (3 tbsp.)
- Minced garlic (1 tbsp.)
- Keto-friendly soy sauce (1 tbsp.)
- Water (1 tbsp.)
- Medium green pepper (1)
- Crushed red pepper (.5 tsp.)
- Squared pork for kebabs (1 lb.)

Prep Technique:

1. Warm up the oven or grill using the broil or the high heat setting.
2. In a processor or blender, combine the water with the red pepper, soy sauce, garlic, butter, and hot sauce.

3. Slice the pork into squares. Cover with the marinade and rest for one hour.
4. Chop the peppers to fit the skewer. Thread the skewers alternating the
pork and peppers.
5. Broil using the high heat setting for five minutes per side.

Pork Carnitas - Instant Pot

Servings Provided: 11
Macro Counts Per Serving:
- **Calories**: 160
- **Protein**: 20 g
- **Fat Content**: 7 g
- **Total Net Carbs**: 1 g

Ingredient List:
- Shoulder blade roast (2.5 lb.) trimmed and boneless
- Kosher salt (2 tsp.)
- Black pepper (as desired)
- Cumin (1.5 tsp.)
- Minced garlic (6 cloves)
- Sazon GOYA (.5 tsp.)
- Dried oregano (.25 tsp.)
- Reduced-sodium chicken broth (.75 cup)
- Bay leaves (2)
- Chipotle peppers in adobo sauce (2-3)
- Dry adobo seasoning – ex. Goya (.25 tsp.)

- Garlic powder (.5 tsp.)

Prep Technique:

1. Prepare the roast with pepper and salt. Sear the roast for about five minutes in a skillet. Let it cool and insert the garlic slivers into the roast using a blade (approximately one-inch deep). Season with the garlic powder, sazon, cumin, oregano, and adobo.

2. Arrange the chicken in the Instant Pot, and add the broth, chipotle peppers, and bay leaves. Stir and secure the lid. Prepare using high pressure for 50 minutes (meat button).

3. Natural release the pressure and shred the pork. Combine with the juices, and trash the bay leaves.

4. Add a bit more cumin and adobo if needed. Stir well and serve.

Pork-Chop Fat Bombs

Servings Provided: 3
Macro Counts Per Serving:
- **Calories**: 1076
- **Protein**: 30 g
- **Fat Content**: 103 g
- **Total Net Carbs**: 7 g

Ingredient List:
- Boneless pork chops (3)
- Oil (.5 cup)
- Medium yellow onion (1)
- Brown mushrooms (8 oz.)
- Nutmeg (1 tsp.)
- Garlic powder (1 tsp.)
- Mayonnaise (1 cup)
- Balsamic vinegar (1 tbsp.)

Prep Technique:
1. Rinse, drain, and slice the mushrooms. Peel and slice the onion. Put them in a large skillet with oil and sauté until wilted.

2. Place the chops to the side and sprinkle using the nutmeg and garlic powder. Cook until done.

3. Transfer the prepared chops onto a plate.

4. Whisk the vinegar and mayonnaise in the pan. The thick sauce can be

thinned with a bit of chicken broth if needed. (Add 2 tablespoons at a time.)

5. Ladle the sauce over the bomb and serve.

Roasted Leg of Lamb

Servings Provided: 2
Macro Counts Per Serving:
- **Calories**: 223
- **Protein**: 22 g
- **Fat Content**: 14 g
- **Total Net Carbs**: 1 g

Ingredient List:
- Reduced-sodium beef broth (.5 cup)
- Leg of lamb (2 lb.)
- Chopped garlic cloves (6)
- Fresh rosemary leaves (1 tbsp.)
- Black pepper (1 tsp.)
- Salt (2 tsp.)

Prep Technique:
1. Grease a baking pan and set the oven temperature to 400° Fahrenheit.
2. Arrange the lamb in the pan and add the broth and seasonings.
3. Roast 30 minutes and lower the heat to 350° Fahrenheit.

4. Continue cooking for about one hour or until done.

5. Let the lamb stand about 20 minutes before slicing to serve.

6. Enjoy with some roasted brussels sprouts and extra rosemary for a tasty
change of pace.

Asian Style Tuna Patties

Servings Provided: 6

Macro Counts Per Serving:

- **Calories**: 145
- **Protein**: 17.7 g
- **Fat Content**: 4.2 g
- **Total Net Carbs**: 3.8 g

Ingredient List:

- Light tuna (2 cans)
- Sesame oil (1 tsp.)
- Keto-friendly bread - reduced-calorie (2 slices) or dried breadcrumbs (.75 cup)
- Egg substitute - ex. Eggbeaters (.25 cup)
- Garlic (1 clove)
- Green onions (3)
- Black pepper (1 tsp.)
- Teriyaki sauce (1 tbsp.)
- Ketchup (1 tbsp.)
- Soy sauce (1 tbsp.)
- Cooking oil spray (as needed)

Prep Technique:
1. Prepare the breadcrumbs. Bake the slices of bread at 200 ° Fahrenheit
until dried out. Put in a blender or food processor to equal ¾ cup.
2. Drain the tuna. Peel and mince the garlic and onions. Mix the egg, tuna,
breadcrumbs, garlic, and green onions in a large bowl.
3. Blend the teriyaki sauce, soy sauce, ketchup, pepper, and sesame oil
into the mixture.
4. Shape the tuna patties into a one-inch thickness.
5. Over medium heat in a greased pan with a bit of nonstick cooking spray, fry each side for approximately 5 minutes.
6. Serve with your favorite side dish.

Baked Tilapia and Cherry Tomatoes

Servings Provided: 2
Macro Counts Per Serving:
- **Calories**: 180
- **Protein**: 23 g
- **Fat Content**: 8 g
- **Total Net Carbs**: 4 g

Ingredient List:
- Butter (2 tsp.)
- Tilapia fillets (2 - 4 oz.)
- Cherry tomatoes (8)
- Pitted black olives (.25 cup)
- Garlic powder (1 tsp.)
- Black pepper (.25 tsp.)
- Paprika (.25 tsp.)
- Salt (.5 tsp.)
- Freshly squeezed lemon juice (1 tbsp.)
- *Optional:* Balsamic vinegar (1 tbsp.)

Prep Technique:
1. Set the oven to reach 375 ° Fahrenheit.

2. Grease a roasting pan and add the butter along with the olives and tomatoes at the bottom.

3. Season the tilapia with the spices (paprika, salt, pepper, and garlic powder). Lastly, add the fish fillets lemon juice.

4. Cover the pan with foil and bake until

Ginger and Sesame Salmon

Servings Provided: 2
Macro Counts Per Serving:
- **Calories**: 370
- **Protein**: 33 g
- **Fat Content**: 23.5 g
- **Total Net Carbs**: 2.5 g

Ingredient List:
- Salmon fillet (1 - 10 oz.)
- Sesame oil (2 tsp.)
- White wine 2 tbsp.)
- Soy sauce (2 tbsp.)
- Minced ginger (1-2 tsp.)
- Rice vinegar (1 tbsp.)
- Sugar-free ketchup (1 tbsp.)
- Fish sauce – ex. Red Boat (1 tbsp.)

Prep Technique:

1. Combine all of the fixings in a plastic container with a tight-fitting lid
(omit the ketchup, oil, and wine for now). Marinade them for about 10 to 15 minutes.
2. On the stovetop, prepare a skillet over high heat and pour in the oil. Add the fish when it's hot, skin side down.
3. Brown both sides for three to four minutes.
4. Add the marinated juices to the pan and let it simmer when the fish is
flipped. Arrange the fish on two dinner plates.
5. Pour in the wine and ketchup to the pan and simmer five minutes until
it's reduced. Serve with your favorite vegetable.

Lemon and Dill Wild-Caught Salmon - Slow-Cooked

Servings Provided: 4
Macro Counts Per Serving:
- **Calories**: 341
- **Protein**: 50 g
- **Fat Content**: 13 g
- **Total Net Carbs**: 2 g

Ingredient List:
- Water (2 cups)
- Wild-caught skin-on salmon (2 lb.)
- Reduced-sodium vegetable broth (1 cup)

- Finely chopped onion (1)
- Thinly sliced lemon (1)
- Pepper and salt (as desired)
- Dill sprigs (3)

Prep Technique:

1. Combine all of the fixings in a slow cooker, with the salmon on the bottom.

2. Prepare using the high setting for two hours. It's done once it flakes easily.

Miso Salmon

Servings Provided: 4
Macro Counts Per Serving:
- **Calories**: 215
- **Protein**: 28.38 g
- **Fat Content**: 9.23 g
- **Total Net Carbs**: 0.78 g

Ingredient List:
- Salmon fillets – skin-on (1.25 lb.)
- White wine (2 tbsp.)
- Sake (3 tbsp.)
- Miso – White suggested (3 tbsp.)
- Kosher salt (as desired)

Prep Technique:

1. Slice the salmon into fillets and sprinkle with the salt. Rest for 30 minutes to help remove some of the moisture. Gently wipe off the salt with a towel with 1 tbsp. of the sake.
2. Mix the white wine, miso, and the rest of the sake in a dish.
3. Pour approximately 1/3 of the marinade in an airtight bowl. Add the
fillets and add the rest of the marinade. Refrigerate for 1 to 2 days.
4. When ready to eat, warm up the oven to 400° Fahrenheit. Cover a baking tin with parchment paper.
5. Scrape away the marinade with your fingers to help prevent burning.
6. Bake 25 minutes and serve.

Zucchini Lasagna With Tofu Ricotta and Walnut

Sauce

Servings Provided: 4

Macro Counts Per Serving:
- **Calories**: 356
- **Protein**: 17 g
- **Fat Content**: 25 g
- **Total Net Carbs**: 10 g

Ingredient List - The Sauce:
- Walnuts - finely ground (1 cup)

- Marinara sauce (divided - 1 jar or 25 oz.)
- Chopped sun-dried tomatoes (.25 cup)

Ingredient List - The Lasagna:
- Zucchini (2)
- Tofu Ricotta (1 batch)
- Nutritional Yeast - optional (2 tbsp.)

Ingredient List - The Ricotta:
- Minced garlic (1 clove)
- Firm tofu (14 oz. firm drained and pressed)
- Olive oil (1 tbsp.)
- Dried basil (1 tbsp.)
- Nutritional yeast (3 tbsp.)
- Lemon juice (1 tbsp.)
- Pepper and salt (as desired)

Prep Technique:
1. Warm up the oven to 375° Fahrenheit.
2. Slice the zucchini with a mandolin (11-inches lengthwise).

3. Prepare the ricotta by pulsing all of the fixings in a food processor until
creamy smooth.
4. Combine the marinara and walnuts with the sun-dried tomatoes
-
reserving ¾ cup for the pan.
5. Prepare a baking pan 7.5x9.5 and add the reserved sauce with a layer of
zucchini. Spread the tofu ricotta over the noodles followed by a sprinkle
of the yeast. Pour about half the walnut sauce on the top
6. Layer until finished and bake for 35 minutes until done.

Dinner Rolls

Servings Provided: 6 rolls
Macro Counts Per Serving:
- **Calories**: 219
- **Protein**: 10.7 g
- **Fat Content**: 18 g
- **Total Net Carbs**: 2.3 g

Ingredient List:
- Mozzarella (1 cup - shredded)
- Cream cheese (1 oz.)
- Almond flour (1 cup)
- Ground flaxseed (.25 cup)
- Egg (1)
- Baking soda (.5 tsp.)

Prep Technique:

1. Warm the oven to reach 400° Fahrenheit.
2. Line a baking tin with a sheet of parchment baking paper.
3. Melt the mozzarella and cream cheese together (microwave for 1 min.).
4. Stir well and add a whisked egg. Combine well.
5. In another container, whisk the baking soda, almond flour, and flaxseed. Mix in the cheese mixture to form a sticky soft-ball.
6. Wet your hands slightly and roll the dough into six balls.
7. Roll the tops of the rolls in sesame seeds and place them on the baking sheet.
8. Bake until nicely browned (10-12 min.).
9. Cool 15 minutes and serve.

Apple Crisp With Blackberries

Servings Provided: 8
Macro Counts Per Serving:
- **Calories**: 200
- **Protein**: 3 g
- **Fat Content**: 16 g
- **Total Net Carbs**: 13 g

Ingredient List - The Topping:
- Chopped pecans (.5 cup)
- Blanched almond flour (.5 cup)
- Confectioners swerve sweetener (.25 cup)
- Salted butter (3 tbsp. melted)
- Ground cinnamon (.5 tsp.)

Ingredient List - The Filling:
- Golden delicious apples (3 small)
- Fresh blackberries (1.25 cups)
- Confectioners swerve sweetener (.25 cup)
- Water (.25 cup)
- Salted butter (2 tbsp.)
- Ground cinnamon (1 tbsp.)
- Vanilla extract (1 tsp.)

- *Also Needed:* Glass 1.5-quart - 9×5-inch loaf pan and a 10-inch nonstick skillet

Prep Technique:

1. Peel and core the apples into eight wedges. Position an oven rack in the center of the oven. Preheat to 350° Fahrenheit.

2. Make the Topping: In a large mixing bowl, add all topping ingredients
except the melted butter, stirring until well-mixed. Add butter and continue stirring until its appearance is that of moistened crumbles. Set
aside.

3. Prepare the Filling: In a skillet, melt butter using medium heat. As it starts to bubble, stir occasionally to avoid burning. Carefully stir in water to cool the butter, adding in the sweetener, cinnamon, and vanilla

until dissolved.

4. Bring to a simmer, and add the apple wedges and blackberries. Cook until most of the released liquid is evaporated, and the softened apples are easily punctured (10 to 15 min.), stirring frequently for even cooking. Turn off the heat.

5. Transfer the filling to a loaf baking dish, spreading out the filling to cover the bottom of the dish. Spread the topping over the filling, breaking up large chunks and making sure the filling is covered by the topping.

6. Transfer the dish to the oven, baking until the topping looks crisp (15 to 20 min.). Let it cool for about 10 minutes before serving.

7. *Note:* Use sweet and crisp varieties such as golden delicious, Honeycrisp, or Braeburn, which better maintain their texture and shape
during cooking.

Blueberry Cupcakes

Servings Provided: 12
Macro Counts Per Serving:
- **Calories**: 138
- **Protein**: 4.4 g
- **Fat Content**: 11.4 g
- **Total Net Carbs**: 2.8 g

Ingredient List:
- Melted butter (1 stick)
- Coconut flour (.5 cup)
- Granulated sweetener of choice (4 tbsp.)
- Baking powder (1 tsp.)
- Lemon juice (2 tbsp.)
- Vanilla (1 tsp.)
- Zest of a lemon (2 tbsp.)
- Eggs (8 medium)
- Fresh blueberries (1 cup)
- *Also Needed:* 12-cupcake holder and liners

Prep Technique:
1. Set the oven temperature to 350° Fahrenheit.

2. Combine the melted butter, sweetener, coconut flour, baking powder,
vanilla, lemon juice, and zest together.

3. Whisk the eggs, adding them in one at a time. Mix well.

4. Taste the cupcake batter to ensure you have used enough sweetener and
flavors to mask the subtle taste of coconut from the coconut flour.

5. Dump the batter into the tins.

6. Press in a few fresh blueberries in the batter of each cupcake.

7. Pop into the oven to bake until golden brown or about 15 minutes.

8. Cover with sugar-free cream cheese frosting. Vanilla or lemon flavor is
perfect. Garnish with fresh blueberries and lemon zest.

9. *Note*: Icing/frosting is additional and optional.

Chocolate-Filled Peanut Butter Cookies

Servings Provided: 20
Macro Counts Per Serving:
- **Calories**: 150
- **Protein**: 4.5 g
- **Fat Content**: 14 g
- **Total Net Carbs**: 2.7 g

Ingredient List:
- Almond flour (2.5 cups)
- Peanut butter (.5 cup)
- Coconut oil (.25 cup)
- Erythritol (.25 cup)
- Maple syrup (3 tbsp.)
- Vanilla extract (1 tbsp.)
- Baking powder (1.5 tsp.)
- Salt (.5 tsp.)
- Dark chocolate bars (2-3)

Prep Technique:
1. Prepare the cookie pan with the paper.
2. Warm up the oven to reach 350° Fahrenheit.

3. Whisk each of the wet fixings together and mix in with the dry ingredients.
4. Mix well and place in the fridge for 20 to 30 minutes.
5. Break the bars into small squares. Shape the dough into little balls until
they are flat.
6. Add one to two pieces of chocolate and seal it into the ball.
7. Arrange on the cookie sheet.
8. Bake for about 15 minutes. Remove and serve.

Creamy Lime Pie

Servings Provided: 8
Macro Counts Per Serving:
- **Calories**: 386
- **Protein**: 7 g
- **Fat Content**: 38.6 g
- **Total Net Carbs**: 4.2 g

Ingredient List:
- Melted butter (.25 cup)
- Almond flour (1.5 cups)
- Erythritol (divided - .5 cup)
- Salt (.5 tsp.)
- Heavy cream (1 cup)
- Egg yolks (4)
- Freshly squeezed key lime juice (.33 cup)
- Lime zest (1 tbsp.)
- Cubed cold butter (.25 cup)
- Vanilla extract (1 tsp.)
- Xanthan gum (.25 tsp.)
- Sour cream (1 cup)
- Cream cheese (.5 cup)

Prep Technique:

1. Warm the oven to reach 350° Fahrenheit.
2. Melt the butter in a pan.
3. Mix the salt, half or .25 cup of erythritol, and almond flour.
4. Slowly add the butter. Blend and press into a pie platter.
5. Bake for 15 minutes. Remove when it's lightly browned. Let it cool.
6. In another saucepan, combine the egg yolks, heavy cream, lime zest, juice, and the remainder of the erythritol.
7. Simmer using the medium heat temperature setting until it starts to thicken (7-10 min.).
8. Take the pan from the heat and add the xanthan gum, vanilla extract, cold butter, cream cheese, and sour cream. Whisk until smooth.
9. Scoop into the cooled pie shell. Cover and place in the fridge.

10. *Note:* You can serve after four hours, but it is better if you wait overnight to enjoy it.

Dark Chocolate Milkshake

Servings Provided: 2
Macro Counts Per Serving:
- **Calories**: 302
- **Protein**: 4.8 g
- **Fat Content**: 27.1 g
- **Total Net Carbs**: 2.5 g

Ingredient List:
- Heavy whipping cream (6 tbsp.)
- Canned coconut milk (5 tbsp.)
- Vanilla extract (.125 tsp.)
- Unsweetened dark cocoa powder (2 tbsp.)
- Stevia sugar substitute or other sugar substitutes (2 tbsp.)

Prep Technique:
1. Use an electric mixer to prepare the cream. Once stiff peaks have formed, add in the rest of the fixings and continue mixing until stiff peaks form again.
2. Put the mixture into the freezer for about 20 minutes.

3. Take the container out of the freezer and stir. Continue the process until
you have reached the desired consistency.

Peanut Butter Cups

Servings Provided: 12
Macro Counts Per Serving:
- **Calories**: 220
- **Protein**: 6 g
- **Fat Content**: 20 g
- **Total Net Carbs**: 2 g

Ingredient List:
- Low-carb milk chocolate (12 oz.)

Ingredient List - Peanut butter mixture:
- Keto-friendly organic peanut butter (3.5 oz.)
- Powdered erythritol (2 tbsp.)
- Whey protein powder (1 oz.)

Prep Technique:
1. Prepare a 12-count muffin tin with paper wrappers.
2. Mix the peanut butter fixings thoroughly, until it becomes a dough that
doesn't stick to the sides of the bowl. For easier handling, refrigerate to

use later.

3. Melt the chocolate in a double boiler using low heat. Remove from heat
once liquid. Pour about 1 tablespoonful into each of the holders.

4. Chill in the refrigerator until firm (15 min.).

5. Take the wrappers and peanut butter out of the refrigerator.

6. Place a .5 tablespoon ball of peanut butter in each wrapper and flatten
until it nearly touches the edge of the wrapper.

7. Stir the remaining liquid chocolate and then pour 4 teaspoonsful of
chocolate over each filled wrapper.

8. Chill in the fridge until hardened or for about 30 minutes.

9. Store at room temperature.

Peanut Butter Pie

Servings Provided:
Macro Counts Per Serving:
- **Calories**: 430
- **Protein**: 8.1 g
- **Fat Content**: 37.4 g
- **Total Net Carbs**: 7.5 g

Ingredient List - The Chocolate Almond Crust:
- Almond flour (1.5 cups)
- Cocoa (.33 cup)
- Sweetener - swerve (.25 cup)
- Melted butter (5 tbsp.)

Ingredient List - The Filling:
- Unchilled cream cheese (24 oz.)
- Smooth, natural peanut butter (.75 cup)
- Pyure Organic Stevia Blend sweetener (.75 cup)
- Whipping cream (1.5 cups)
- Cream of tartar (.5 tsp.)

Prep Technique:

1. Unchill the cream cheese on the countertop for about two hours before
you begin.
2. Prepare the crust. Mix and press into a springform 9-inch pan and bake
at 400° Fahrenheit for 8-10 minutes.
3. In another container, whisk the sweetener and whipping cream. Mix in
the cream of tartar.
4. In another mixing container, combine the cream cheese and nut butter.
5. Combine the mixtures and fill the pan into the crust.
6. Chill for 30-45 minutes in the freezer or for 3 to 4 hours in the fridge
7. Dust with crushed peanuts and cocoa before serving.

Pecan Pie Clusters

Servings Provided: 10 clusters

Macro Counts Per Serving:

- **Calories**: 140
- **Protein**: 1 g
- **Fat Content**: 14 g
- **Total Net Carbs**: 1 g

Ingredient List:

- Chopped pecans (1 cup)
- Dark or sugar-free chocolate (2 oz. - chopped)
- Butter (3 tbsp.)
- Heavy cream (.25 cup)
- Zen Sweet or sweetener of choice (2 tbsp.)
- Vanilla (1 tsp.)

Prep Technique:

1. Using the medium temperature setting, brown the butter until golden.
Stir frequently.

2. Once golden, add heavy cream and whisk together. Turn down heat to a
simmer. Whisk in the sweetener and vanilla, working until it's lumpfree.
3. Whisk occasionally for the next five minutes. (The mixture will have a
consistency similar to caramel and slightly darken.) Remove from the heat.
4. Mix in the chopped pecans and spoon the clusters onto a parchmentlined
tray. Place in the freezer for five minutes.
5. Microwave dark chocolate for 20-40 seconds until melted and smooth.
Drizzle over the clusters and enjoy.

Pumpkin Cheesecake

Servings Provided: 12
Macro Counts Per Serving:
- **Calories**: 346
- **Protein**: 6 g
- **Fat Content**: 33 g
- **Total Net Carbs**: 4 g

Ingredient List - Walnut Crust:
- Walnuts (2 cups)
- Butter, melted (3 tbsp.)
- Cinnamon (1 tsp.)
- Vanilla (.5 tsp.)
- *Optional:* Sweetener (2 tsp.)

Ingredient List - Cheesecake Fluff:
- Cream cheese (16 oz. - softened)
- Powdered swerve (1 cup)
- Heavy whipping cream (.66 cup)
- Pumpkin puree (.66 cup)
- Pumpkin spice (2 tsp.)
- Vanilla (1 tsp.)

Prep Technique:

1. Warm the oven to 350° Fahrenheit.

2. Combine all of the crust fixings in a food processor until it has a doughlike

consistency, scraping down the sides as needed.

3. Press the dough into a 9-inch round baking dish. Bake for 12-15 minutes until lightly brown.

4. Remove and let cool for 20 minutes.

5. Prepare the pumpkin fluff. In a large bowl, whip softened cream cheese, heavy whipping cream and swerve together until fluffy (hand mixer or stand mixers works best)

6. Add the pumpkin puree, pumpkin spice, and vanilla. Beat until combined.

7. Spread cheesecake fluff on the cooled walnut crust and refrigerate until

set or for at least two hours.

Walnut Cookies

Servings Provided: 16
Macro Counts Per Serving:
- **Calories**: 72
- **Protein**: 3 g
- **Fat Content**: 6.7 g
- **Total Net Carbs**: 1.1 g

Ingredient List:
- Egg (1)
- Ground cinnamon (1 tsp.)
- Erythritol (2 tbsp.)
- Ground walnuts (1.5cups)

Prep Technique:

1. Warm the oven to reach 350° Fahrenheit. Prepare a baking tin with a
sheet of parchment baking paper.
2. Combine the cinnamon and erythritol with the egg. Fold in the walnuts.
3. Shape into balls and bake for 10 to 13 minutes. Cool slightly and serve.

Zucchini Spiced Cupcakes

Servings Provided: 12
Macro Counts Per Serving:
- **Calories**: 68
- **Protein**: 4.9 g
- **Fat Content**: 23.1 g
- **Total Net Carbs**: 3.5 g

Ingredient List- The Cakes:
- Almond flour (1 cup)
- Coconut flour (.33 - .5 cup)
- Xanthan gum (.5 tsp.)
- Bak. soda (1 tsp.)
- Bak. powder (.5 tsp.)
- Salt (.5 tsp.)
- Cinnamon (1 tsp.)
- Ground cloves (.125 tsp.)
- Nutmeg (.25 tsp.)
- Coconut oil liquefied (.5 cup)
- Large eggs (2 unchilled)
- Sugar-free vanilla extract (1.5 tsp.)
- Monk fruit sweetener (1 cup)
- Packed grated zucchini (1.5 cups)

- *Optional:* Walnuts coarsely chopped

Ingredient List - The Frosting:
- Softened cream cheese (4 oz.)
- Butter (2 tbsp. softened)
- Monk fruit sweetener - powdered (.5 cup)
- Vanilla extract (.5 tsp.)
- *Also Needed*: Electric mixer or food processor

Prep Technique:

1. Warm the oven in advance to reach 350° Fahrenheit.

2. Sift both flours together. Prepare the muffin tins with paper or foil baking liners.

3. Stir in both types of flour with the baking soda, xanthan gum, baking powder, nutmeg, cinnamon, salt, and cloves. Set aside for now.

4. Whisk the coconut oil, eggs, and vanilla extract. Stir in zucchini and

sweetener, and the flour mixture. Fold in the walnuts. Add the batter to
the liners.

5. Bake until the cake is firm to touch (25-30 min.).

6. Remove cool on a rack. Frost with cream cheese frosting if desired.

7. Store cupcakes in the refrigerator or freezer.

8. Cool to reach room temperature before serving.

Preparation Steps - The Frosting:

1. Pour the sweetener in a blender.

2. Mix the butter and cream cheese until fully incorporated.

3. Add the vanilla and frost the cake.

Blueberry Cream Cheese Bombs

Servings Provided: 24
Macro Counts Per Serving:
- **Calories**: 116
- **Protein**: .44 g
- **Fat Content**: 13 g
- **Total Net Carbs**: 1.02 g

Ingredient List:
- Scant blueberries (1 cup)
- Coconut oil (.75 cup)
- Butter (1 stick)
- Coconut cream (.25 cup)
- Softened cream cheese (4 oz.)
- Sweetener of choice

Prep Technique:
1. Arrange three or four berries in each mold cup.
2. Melt the coconut oil and butter over the lowest stovetop heat setting.
Cool slightly for approximately five minutes.

3. Combine all of the ingredients and whisk well. Slowly, add the sweetener.
4. Using a spouted pitcher, fill an ice tray with 24 bombs.
5. Pop them out and eat when hunger strikes.

Chocolate Chip Cheesecake Fat Bombs

Servings Provided: 12
Macro Counts Per Serving:
- **Calories**: 112
- **Protein**: 1 g
- **Fat Content**: 12 g
- **Total Net Carbs**: 1 g

Ingredient List:
- Unchilled cream cheese - softened (4 oz.)
- Melted butter (4 tbsp.)
- Coconut oil (.25 cup)
- Sweetener ex. Lakanto Monkfruit (2 tbsp.)
- Chocolate chips- ex. Lily's sweetened with stevia (.25 cup)
- Vanilla extract (1 tsp.)

Prep Technique:
1. Prepare a mini cupcake pan with or without liners
2. Combine the melted butter, cream cheese, coconut oil, sweetener, and

vanilla extract in a mixing container.
3. Using a hand mixer, blend for two
to three minutes until smooth.
4. Fold in the chocolate chips,
holding a few to add as a garnish to
each
bomb as desired.
5. Scoop the mixture into the muffin
tin.
6. Freeze for 30 minutes. Remove
from the tray and serve.

Cocoa Butter Walnut Fat Bombs

Servings Provided: 8
Macro Counts Per Serving:
- **Calories**: 265
- **Protein**: 0.9 g
- **Fat Content**: 20 g
- **Total Net Carbs**: 0.3 g

Ingredient List:
- Coconut oil (4 tbsp.)
- Erythritol (4 tbsp. powdered)
- Butter (4 tbsp.)
- Cocoa butter (4 oz.)
- Chopped walnuts (.5 cup)
- Vanilla extract (.5 tsp.)
- Salt (.25 tsp)

Prep Technique:

1. Prepare a pan using the medium-high temperature setting on the stovetop. Add the butter, coconut oil, and cocoa butter.

2. Once it's melted, add the walnuts, salt, stevia, vanilla extract, and erythritol. Mix well.

3. Pour into the silicone mold. Store the treats in the refrigerator for one hour before serving.

Lemon Cheesecake Fat Bombs

Servings Provided: 16
Macro Counts Per Serving:
- **Calories**: 60
- **Protein**: 1 g
- **Fat Content**: 7 g
- **Total Net Carbs**: 0.5 g

Ingredient List:
- Cream cheese (6 oz. - note that each brick is 8 oz.)
- Salted butter (4 tbsp.)
- Granular swerve sweetener (1.5 oz. /3 tbsp.)
- Fresh lemon juice (2 tbsp.)
- *Optional*: Finely grated lemon zest (1 tbsp.)
- *Also Needed*: Silicone molds

Prep Technique:
1. Let the cream cheese and butter sit at room temperature until softened
before continuing with the recipe.

2. Whisk the sweetener, lemon juice, and lemon zest. Whisk until wellmixed.

3. In another bowl, microwave the cream cheese until very soft (10 sec.).

4. Add the cream cheese and butter to the bowl with the lemon juice mixture. Use an electric hand mixer (low speed) to beat until wellmixed.

5. Divide the batter into the molds. Freeze for several hours until solid before serving.

6. Store the leftovers in the freezer.

Orange and Walnut Chocolate Fat Bombs

Servings Provided: 8
Macro Counts Per Serving:
- **Calories**: 87
- **Protein**: 1 g
- **Fat Content**: 9 g
- **Total Net Carbs**: 2 g

Ingredient List:
- 85% Cocoa dark chocolate (12.5 grams)
- Extra-Virgin coconut oil (.25 cup)
- Orange peel or orange extract (.5 tbsp.)
- Walnuts (1.75 cups)
- Cinnamon (1 tsp.)
- Stevia (10-15 drops)

Prep Technique:
1. Use the microwave, or a saucepan to melt the chocolate. Add cinnamon
and coconut oil. Sweeten mixture with stevia.

2. Pour in the fresh orange peel and chopped walnuts.

3. In a muffin tin or in candy mold, spoon in the mixture.

4. Place in the refrigerator for one to three hours until the mixture is solid.

Healthy Snack Options
Almond Coconut Bars

Servings Provided: 6
Macro Counts Per Serving:
- **Calories**: 253
- **Protein**: 5 g
- **Fat Content**: 25 g
- **Total Net Carbs**: 2 g

Ingredient List:
- Coconut oil (.5 cup)
- Almond flour (1.25 cups)
- Coconut flour (.25 cup
- Eggs (2)
- Sugar substitute (3 tbsp.)
- Almond butter (2 tbsp.)
- Salt (.25 tsp.)
- Water (1 cup)
- Vanilla extract (1 tsp.)
- *Also Needed:* Baking pan and Trivet for the Instant Pot

Prep Technique:
1. Line the pan that fits in the cooker with the baking paper.

2. Combine all of the fixings in the food processor. Empty into the pan.
3. Empty the water into the Instant Pot with the steamer rack. Arrange the
pan in the cooker and secure the lid.
4. Set the timer for 15 minutes.
5. Natural-release the pressure and chill the pan until its room temperature.
6. Slice into six bars.

Bacon Guacamole Fat Bombs

Servings Provided: 6
Macro Counts Per Serving:
- **Calories**: 156
- **Protein**: 3.4 g
- **Fat Content**: 15.2 g
- **Total Net Carbs**: 1.4 g

Ingredient List:
- Avocado (.5 of large or 3.5 oz.)
- Bacon (4 strips)
- Butter or ghee (.25 cup)
- Garlic cloves (2 crushed)
- Diced onion (.5 of 1 small)
- Finely chopped chili pepper (1 small)
- Fresh lime juice (1 tbsp.)
- Salt (to your liking)
- Ground black pepper or cayenne (1 pinch)
- Freshly chopped cilantro (1-2 tbsp.)

Prep Technique:

1. Program the oven setting to 375° Fahrenheit.
2. Line the tray with parchment paper and cook the bacon for ten to fifteen
minutes. Save the grease for step four.
3. Peel, deseed, and chop the avocado into a dish along with the garlic,
chili pepper, lime juice, cilantro, black pepper, salt, and butter.
4. Use a fork or potato masher to combine the mixture and blend in the
onion.
5. Empty the grease into the bomb, blend well, and cover for 20 to 30 minutes in the refrigerator. Make six balls.
6. Break up the bacon into a bowl and roll the balls in it until coated evenly and serve for breakfast or a snack.

Spicy Deviled Eggs

Servings Provided: 6
Macro Counts Per Serving:
- **Calories**: 200
- **Protein**: 6 g
- **Fat Content**: 19 g
- **Total Net Carbs**: 1 g

Ingredient List:
- Eggs (6)
- Mayonnaise (.5 cup)
- Red curry paste (1 tbsp.)
- Poppy seeds (.5 tbsp.)

- Salt (.25 tsp.)

Prep Technique:

1. Prepare a pan with just enough water to cover the eggs. Do *not* put a lid
on the pot but bring it to a boil.
2. Cook the eggs for about 8 minutes. Place into an ice water bath at that
time.
3. Discard the eggshells and cut the eggs in half. Scoop out the egg yolk.
4. Place the whites on a platter and place it in the fridge.
5. Combine the mayonnaise, curry paste, and egg yolks until smooth.
6. Take the egg whites from the fridge and apply the prepared yolks. Sprinkle with the seeds on top to serve._

Instant Pot Chicken Adobo

Servings Provided: 4
Macro Counts Per Serving:
- **Calories**: 370
- **Protein**: 37 g
- **Fat Content**: 21 g
- **Total Net Carbs**: 6.5g

Ingredient List:
- Chicken thighs (2 - 2.5 lb.)
- Low-sodium soy sauce (.5 cup)
- White vinegar (.33 cup)
- Sliced onion (1)

- Garlic (5 minced cloves)
- Bay leaves (3)
- Olive oil (2 tbsp.)
- Cayenne (.25 tsp.)
- Salt and coarse black pepper (to your liking)

Ingredient List - For Serving - Optional:

- Scallions (2 sliced)
- Cooked cauliflower rice

Prep Technique:

1. Select the sauté function on the Instant Pot.
2. Remove the skin and bones from the chicken. Generously season chicken thighs using the pepper and salt.
3. Pour the oil into the pot.
4. Arrange half of the chicken thighs in the pot and sauté for a couple of minutes per side Place on a platter and continue the process until done.

5. Pour in the vinegar, soy sauce, garlic, onion, and cayenne. Stir well and
scrape any browned bits in the pot.
6. Add the chicken in a single layer, placing them on top of the onions, and toss in the bay leaves. Securely close the lid.
7. Cook for 10 minutes using the high-pressure function. Quick-release
the steam and switch to the sauté function. Toss the bay leaves.
8. Sauté for another 15 minutes to thicken the sauce.
9. Serve the chicken and sauce, with cooked cauliflower rice and scallions.

Pan-Glazed Chicken and Basil

Servings Provided: 4

Macro Counts Per Serving:
- **Calories**: 161
- **Protein**: 26.2 g
- **Fat Content**: 4.7 g
- **Total Net Carbs**: 4.6 g

Ingredient List:
- Chicken breast halves (4- 4-oz.)
- Balsamic vinegar (2 tbsp.)
- Olive oil (2 tsp.)

- Dried Basil (2 tsp.)
- Black pepper and salt (.25 tsp. each)
- Honey (1 tbsp.)

Prep Technique:

1. Spice up the chicken with sea salt for a coarser salt. You can also add pepper.

2. Place the chicken in a large pan with oil using a med-high burner for about 4 or 5 minutes on each side.

3. Flip the chicken, and simmer for an extra five minutes or so. Mix and pour the vinegar, basil, and honey over the chicken. Continue cooking for 1 minute.

Slow-Cooked Teriyaki

Servings Provided: 6
Macro Counts Per Serving:
- **Calories**: 158
- **Protein**: 20 g
- **Fat Content**: 6 g
- **Total Net Carbs**: 4 g

Ingredient List:
- Chicken thighs (2 lb.)
- Red pepper (2)
- Yellow onion (1)
- Garlic cloves (3)
- Reduced-sodium beef broth (.5 cup)

- Coconut aminos (.25 cup)
- Water (.33 cup)
- Knob freshly grated ginger (1-inch piece)
- Pepper and salt (as desired)
- For the Garnish: 4 green onions
- Optional for Serving: Lettuce leaves

Prep Technique:

1. Chop the peppers, onions, and garlic.

2. Whisk the water, aminos, and broth – adding it to the cooker.

3. Blend in the rest of the fixings (omit the lettuce and green onions).

4. Cook for six hours using the high heat setting.

5. When done; garnish with onions, as is, or, on a bed of lettuce to create a
delicious taco.

Thai Green Chicken Curry Instant Pot

Servings Provided: 6
Macro Counts Per Serving:
- **Calories**: 231
- **Protein**: 17 g
- **Fat Content**: 15 g
- **Total Net Carbs**: 5 g

Ingredient List:
- Chicken thighs – remove skin and bones (1 lb.)
- Curry paste (2 tbsp.)
- Coconut oil (1 tbsp.)
- Minced garlic (1 tbsp.)
- Minced ginger (1 tbsp.)

- Sliced onion (.5 cup)
- Basil leaves (.5 cup)
- Peeled – chopped eggplant (2 cups)
- Chopped yellow, green or orange pepper (1)
- Unsweetened coconut milk (1 cup)
- Splenda/another sweetener (2 tbsp.)
- Soy sauce/coconut aminos (2 tbsp.)
- Salt (1 tbsp.)
- Fish sauce (1 tbsp.)

Prep Technique:

1. Set the Instant Pot on the sauté function. When hot, add the oil, and curry paste. Sauté for one to two minutes.

2. Toss in the garlic and ginger. Sauté for about 30 seconds. Stir in the
onions along with the rest of the fixings. Deglaze the pan.

3. Switch to the slow cooker mode for 8 hours using the medium setting.
4. Stir and enjoy!

Bacon Burger and Cabbage Stir Fry

Servings Provided: 10
Macro Counts Per Serving:
- **Calories**: 357
- **Protein**:31.9 g
- **Fat Content**: 21.9 g
- **Total Net Carbs**: 4.5 g

Ingredient List:
- Ground beef (1 lb.)
- Bacon (1 lb.)
- Small onion (1)
- Cloves of garlic (3)
- Small head of cabbage (1 lb.)

- Black pepper (.25 tsp.)
- Sea salt (.5 tsp.)

Prep Technique:

1. Chop the bacon and onion. Mince the garlic.

2. Combine the beef and bacon in a wok or large skillet. Prepare until done and store in a bowl to keep warm.

3. Toss the minced garlic and onion into the hot grease. Add the cabbage and stir-fry until wilted. Blend in the meat and combine. Sprinkle with the pepper and salt as desired. Serve.

Barbacoa Beef

Servings Provided: 9
Macro Counts Per Serving:
- **Calories**: 153
- **Protein**: 24 g
- **Fat Content**: 4.5 g
- **Total Net Carbs**: 2 g

Ingredient List:
- Med. onion (.5 of 1)
- Garlic (5 cloves)
- Chipotles in adobo sauce (2-4)
- Lime (1 juiced)
- Cumin (1 tbsp.)
- Oregano (1 tbsp.)

- Water (1 cup)
- Ground cloves (.5 tsp.)
- Bay leaves (3)
- Kosher salt (2.5 tsp.)
- Black pepper (as desired)
- Eye of round/bottom round (3 lb.)
- Oil (1 tsp.)

Prep Technique:

1. In a blender, puree the onion, garlic cloves, lime juice, water, cloves,
chipotles, cumin, and oregano – until smooth.

2. Remove all fat from the meat and chop into 3-inch bits. Season with 2 teaspoons of salt and a pinch of pepper.

3. Prepare an Instant Pot using the sauté setting and add the oil. Brown the
meat in batches (5 min.). Add the sauce from the blender, and the bay leaves into the Instant Pot.

4. Secure the lid and set the timer for 65 minutes using the high-pressure
setting. Natural or quick release the pressure and shred the beef with two forks. Reserve the juices and throw the bay leaves in the trash.
5. Return the meat to the pot with the cumin, salt to taste, and 1.5 cups of
the reserved juices. Serve when hot.